Living with Llamas

Written by Janine Scott
Photography by Victor Englebert

Peru

Most people in Peru live in cities or towns. Luisa and her family live in a small village in the Andes highlands. She and the other children go to school and help their parents with the daily chores. The children also share the responsibility of taking care of the herds of llamas and alpacas.

responsibility being trusted with something

Contents

Living with Llamas

My name is Luisa. I live in the highlands
of the Andes Mountains in Peru. I live with
my mother, father, and four brothers and sisters.
We speak Quechua, which was the language
of the Inca.

Inca an ancient civilization of South America

Why do you think there are no trees where Luisa lives?

Our village is 15,000 feet above sea level. At this altitude, many people find it hard to breathe until they get used to it. It is very cold in the mountains. There are no trees where we live. Our village is surrounded by rocks, grass, and very steep hills. There is often ice on the ground, too.

altitude the height of a place above the ground

My family has a herd of llamas and alpacas. They are very important to us. I have helped take care of them since I was five years old. When I am not at school, I am responsible for them. I watch the herd while they eat. I make sure that predators, such as pumas, foxes, and condors, do not attack the babies. I also run after animals that wander away from the herd. At night, we lead the herd into stone corrals to keep them safe.

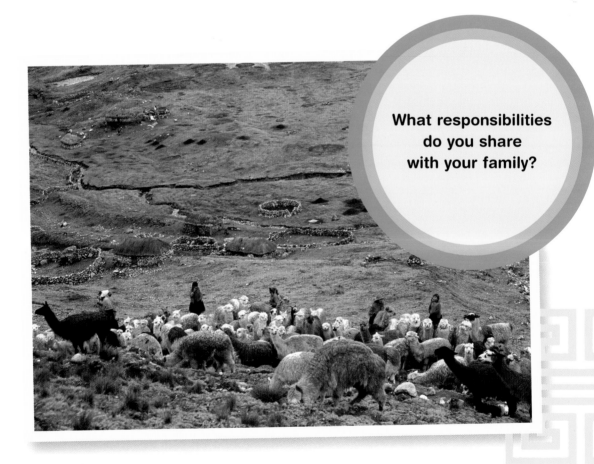

What responsibilities do you share with your family?

corral a pen for animals on a farm or ranch

Llamas and alpacas
often lie back-to-back
so that they can
watch out for danger
sneaking up on them.

We spend a lot of time weaving. We use the thick wool from our llamas to make blankets, bags, and ropes. We use the fine wool from our alpacas to make clothes and hats. First, we spin the wool into yarn. We often do this while we walk with the herd or at the end of the day. We color the alpaca wool yarn with vegetable dyes.

Old Ways, Old Days

Some local women in the highlands still wear felt hats, full skirts, and shawls around their shoulders. The shawls are useful for carrying things. This style of clothing was worn in the past.

We weave the wool yarn on wooden looms. I often weave as I look after the herd. Clothes made out of wool help keep us warm in the cold mountains. The patterns we weave are handed down from mother to daughter.

Cochineal are insects that live on prickly pear cactuses. The insects produce a red dye called carmine. For centuries, people from Peru have used carmine to dye their clothes.

loom a machine used for weaving thread into cloth

Our village has a schoolhouse. We learn math and Spanish. Our teacher goes back home once a month. It takes her three days on a horse.

Some of my aunts, uncles, and cousins live in our village. Our stone huts have grass roofs, but they have no windows and no chimneys.

10

Our village gets fresh drinking water from the lakes, rivers, and ponds on the mountain. The water is very cold, but it tastes good.

We grow all the food that we need. We eat potatoes, maize, and oca. We grow many different kinds of potatoes at different levels of the mountain. We have huts down where we grow our vegetables. We stay in the huts for weeks at a time while we plant and harvest our crops. It takes us nine hours to walk down to where we grow our corn. Our animals carry the food back up the mountain.

Thousands of years ago, potatoes grew wild in Peru. The early peoples learned how to plant and grow potatoes and corn. Today, there are more than 200 kinds of potatoes!

oca   a plant with an edible root that is grown in South America

Did You Know?

It is believed that the white potato first came from Peru, Chile, and Bolivia in South America. The Inca cultivated potatoes in the valleys of the Andes Mountains.

In the mid-1500s, Spanish explorers took the potato back with them to Europe.

The potato was introduced to England, Scotland, and Ireland. The white potato grew well in Ireland. Called the Irish potato, it became the main part of the Irish diet.

cultivate to grow as a crop

 Explore Peru

Peru is in western South America. It has a long chain of mountains running down the country. Jungles lie to the east of these mountains. The land that borders the Pacific Ocean is hot, dry desert.

Peru is the third largest country in South America. Nearly half the people of Peru trace their ancestry back to the ancient Inca empire. Today, most people live in busy cities and towns. Some people still live in rural areas and follow the old ways, like Luisa and her family.

In Peru, most children between six and twelve years old go to school. Schooling is considered highly important.

ancestry   a person's ancestors

Lima is the capital city of Peru. It is home to the oldest university in South America.

On the Go!

What is the city of Lima also known as?
Go to page 16

What metals are mined in Peru?
Go to page 20

Which plant are the floating islands in Lake Titicaca made from?
Go to page 22

PERU

SOUTH AMERICA

PACIFIC OCEAN

Lima ✪

The City of Lima

Lima was once known as the "city of the kings." It was founded in 1535 by the Spanish explorer Francisco Pizarro. Back then, Peru became a colony of Spain. The influence of the Spanish can be seen everywhere in the city. There are plazas, or main squares, surrounded by historic, Spanish-style buildings as well as modern buildings. Today, many of these Spanish buildings are museums, government offices, and restaurants.

colony   a country or an area that is ruled by another country

Soccer is the most popular sport in Peru. All over the cities and towns, groups of children practice wherever and whenever they can. Lima has a stadium that seats 70,000 soccer fans!

The Inca Empire

The Inca empire was a large and advanced ancient civilization in South America. The Inca were skilled engineers who built roads, bridges, buildings, temples, and cities, such as Machu Picchu (MAH choo PEEK choo). The Inca were also famous for their metalwork, weaving, and pottery. They made many objects out of gold, silver, and copper. Some of these treasures can be seen in Peru's museums.

Machu Picchu

empire   a country or a group of countries that have the same ruler

Music of the Inca

The music of Peru is now very popular around the world. Bamboo reed flutes, harps, and drums help create a special sound from the Andes. Long ago, traditional drums were made from hollow tree trunks. Llama hide was stretched across the trunk.

Today, tourists walk the Inca trail and visit Machu Picchu and other ancient ruins. Many tourists are amazed at the skills shown by people who lived long ago.

Open for Business

Peru's economy has been growing since the 1990s. Some of its new and important industries are mining, fishing, and tourism. Peru is rich in silver, copper, and gold. Thousands of tourists come to Peru every year to soak up its history and enjoy its festivals and sporting events.

Peru mines salt at the world-famous Maras salt flats. Salt water comes from a hot stream at the top of the valley and flows into these large basins, or flats. When the water evaporates, the salt is left over.

economy   the way a country makes and consumes goods

Fishing is a leading industry in Peru. The government controls Peru's fishing grounds to help prevent overfishing. Fishing vessels from other countries are charged a fee to fish in Peru's waters.

Farming is a main industry in Peru. Alpacas and llamas have lived in Peru for centuries. They provided meat and wool. Today, Peru's farming industry also exports these animals to other farming countries.

Lake Titicaca

Lake Titicaca is the highest navigable lake in the world. Many islands lie in the lake and along its shores. The Uro-Aymara Indians live on floating islands in the center of the lake. They make their homes and boats from the totara reeds that grow along the shoreline. The islands they live on are made entirely from reeds, too. Fresh reeds must be laid down daily to keep the islands from sinking.

navigable   able to be sailed on by boats and ships

The island of Taquile lies in Lake Titicaca. It is famous for its woolen crafts. The women spin and dye the wool, and the men knit bright garments such as hats, vests, and belts.

Reed boats are often used to transport reeds to the floating islands. Tourists who visit these islands buy crafts such as miniature reed boats as souvenirs.

What Do You Think?

1   Which tasks would you find difficult if you went to stay with Luisa in her mountain village?

2   Why do you think Luisa's family has to walk nine hours down the mountain to where they grow their corn?

How might living with llamas teach Luisa about responsibility?

Index